D0646543

ANCIENT EGYPTIAN PLACES

by Sarah McNeill

The Millbrook Press
Brookfield, Connecticut

For Tobie

Published in the United States in 1997 by

The Millbrook Press
2 Old New Milford Road
Brookfield, Connecticut 06084

First published in Great Britain in 1996 by

Wayland Publishers Ltd. incorporating MacDonald Young Books
61 Western Road
Hove
East Sussex
BN3 1JD

Designed by Neil Adams
Illustrations by Philip McNeill
Consultant: Joanna Defrates

Text copyright © 1996 Sarah McNeill
Illustrations copyright © Philip McNeill

Typeset by DP Press Ltd, Sevenoaks, Kent

Printed and bound by Proost International Book Co., Belgium

Library of Congress Cataloging-in-Publication Data

McNeill, Sarah
Ancient Egyptian places / Sarah McNeill
　　p.　cm.
Includes bibliographical references and index.
Summary: Describes thirteen places around which life in ancient Egypt revolved and how these places fit into the society of the time.

ISBN 0-7613-0057-0 (lib. bdg.)
1. Egypt--Civilization--To 332 B.C. --Juvenile literature.
[1. Egypt--Civilization--To 332 B.C.] I Title
DT61.H66 1997
932--dc20   96-1865
                                                                              CIP
                                                                              AC

Picture Acknowledgments

Picture research by Image Select, London

Front cover: Image Select, London; Spine: Image Select, London; AKG: p 11; Ancient Art & Architecture Collection: pp 9, 27, 28, 32, 35, 36, 39, 40, 41, 44, 45; Ann Ronan Picture Library: pp 16, 17, 29, 37; Bridgeman Art Library: Title page, pp 14, 31; Image Select, London: pp 30, 34; Images Colour Library: pp 18, 20; Spectrum Colour Library: Contents page, pp 6, 19, 25, 26, 38; Werner Forman Archive: pp 10, 15, 22, 23, 24, 42, 43; Zefa: pp 7, 8, 12, 13, 21, 33

CONTENTS

INTRODUCTION

In about 3000 B.C., one of the world's first great civilizations grew up in Egypt, on the banks of the Nile River. Almost everything about the Egyptians was record-breaking in some way. Their kings, or pharaohs, were wealthier and more powerful than other rulers of the time. Their religion was full of magic and drama, with more than 2,000 strange gods and goddesses. Their

artists and craftsmen set to work to honor pharaoh and the gods and produced some of the largest, most impressive buildings the world has ever known. Their fields produced abundant crops, providing more than enough food for all.

In this book, you can visit all sorts of places that were important to the Egyptians, from the homes they lived in while they were alive, to the pyramids and tombs they built to live in when they were dead. You can find out about how the Egyptians lived and worked – whether they were rich and important, such as pharaoh and his nobles; or people who had to work for their living, such as peasants, traders, and craftsmen. You can also find out about their extraordinary and exotic religion, to put together a detailed picture of how the Egyptians created their record-breaking world.

THE RIVER

When ancient Egyptians wanted to praise someone as much as they could, there was only one option. They said the person was as important as the Nile River. That was exactly what one nobleman said to praise his pharaoh, Akhenaten (1353–1335 B.C.):

You are like the River Nile, making Egypt live.

Egypt, gift of the Nile

Everyone in the ancient world knew that Egypt depended on the Nile River. As a desert land, with little rainfall, Egypt needed water from the Nile for farming and food. When a famous ancient Greek named Herodotus visited Egypt, he was especially struck by this. He declared, *"Egypt … is the gift of the Nile."* He meant that without the Nile, life in Egypt would have been impossible. Historians have repeated his words ever since.

The Nile River was Egypt's main "highway." Boats were by far the easiest way to travel. Those going up river could use sails, because winds blowing from the north helped to propel them. But going downstream meant hard work – all hands on the oars.

Making the "Black Land"

Each year between July and October, the Nile River flooded its banks, following heavy rains in the south. A carpet of black fertile mud was deposited all over the land surrounding the Nile. When the flood ebbed away, the mud was left behind. It was just right for growing crops. The Egyptians' name for this fertile strip of country bordering the Nile was "Kemet," meaning the "Black Land." For them, Kemet was a symbol of life and well-being.

Because the Nile was so vital, people worried about it. What if the flood was too high? People and cattle would be swept away, crops would be lost, buildings would be destroyed. But then again, what if the flood was too low? There would be famine. To combat these problems, the Egyptians did their best to control the Nile flood. Before 3100 B.C. a complicated irrigation system of canals and earth banks was built. These banks divided the land into pockets. As the level of water in the Nile rose, the canals channeled the extra water to the land, where the banks trapped it and its fertile mud. When the floods subsided, the water drained off.

Farming scenes painted in an Egyptian tomb. Egyptian farmers relied totally on the Nile River for water.

Trying to control the Nile was a major effort, involving all the community. People from different places had to cooperate with each other, and a strong source of power grew up to direct operations – the royal power of the pharaohs.

The heart of life

There are many ways of telling how important the Nile was to the Egyptians. For example, they devised a calendar that referred to the Nile flood. They divided the year up into three seasons, each lasting four months: inundation (flooding), planting and harvest. There are also all sorts of royal records that mention the Nile flood, classifying it as one of the most important events of the year. *"Nile flood this year, 3 cubits, 5 hands, 2 fingers [6.5 feet or 1.98 meters],"* one record proclaimed, recording the flood along with other major news items – such as wars, religious festivals, and making new statues of the gods.

The Nile was at the heart of Egyptian life in practical ways. Important towns and cities, like Thebes, were built along the river's edge. The Nile provided a great highway through the kingdom for boats and boatmen. It was always busy with all kinds of craft, from little papyrus (reed) canoes belonging to fishermen, to large boats loaded with stone for building or grain for storage. It provided food – *"every kind of fish,"* as one Greek writer put it. Groups of people went out on the river to catch herons, cranes, and wild fowl such as ducks, and to hunt the wildlife that lived in the swampy thickets – hippopotamus and mongoose, for instance.

Models of fishing boats, made for an Egyptian tomb. Models such as these give us a good deal of information about what Egyptian boats looked like and how they worked. But we do not just have to rely on models for our information. King Khufu (2551–2528 B.C.) had a full-sized ship buried in a pit next to his pyramid. It was more than 131 feet (40 meters) long.

The heart of death

The Nile featured in Egyptian religion, too. Egyptians believed a god called Hapy poured the river water out from a water pot. It also had a part to play when pharaoh died. Royal tombs such as the pyramids were usually built on sites on the west bank of the Nile. When pharaoh died, a boat carried his body for burial. The Egyptians believed pharaoh would then be transferred to a different boat, a heavenly boat, to spend eternity with the sun god Re, sailing across the heavens.

THE FIELD

The words of a peasant who lived in ancient Egypt tell us what country people spent their time thinking about – crops and animals. He advised a friend:

I have seen a good donkey – a really good donkey. You must get it. Its face is one of the best.

Muscle power, donkey power and labor-saving devices

Peasants with one of ancient Egypt's most hi-tech farming aids – a donkey. Donkeys were used for carrying heavy loads, such as the baskets of grain shown here, and also for other farm work.

Nearly all farm work had to be done by hand. The farmer's first job for the year was preparing the field for crops. Here he had hoes and plows to help. Then it was time to sow wheat and barley – another job done by hand. It was the same at harvest time, when everyone had to lend a hand: men, women and children. They worked in rows, cutting the stalks of grain with curved knives called sickles.

The Black Land of the Nile produced all kinds of fruit. Here, we can see men crushing grapes with their bare feet. Look how they hold on to ropes to keep their balance. The man at the right is filling jars with grape juice from a tap.

Peasants who worked in the fields would have been overjoyed to see their friend arrive with the donkey mentioned at the beginning of this chapter. In this constant round of hard work, donkeys were one of the farmer's greatest labor-saving devices. Known to the Egyptians – as well as to Winnie the Pooh! – as "eeyore," a donkey was often brought to the fields to work. It carried all sorts of heavy loads, especially sheaves of wheat and barley at harvest time. Donkeys helped at the start of the farming year, too, pulling the plow through the fields. Oxen were also used for this. Once the harvest was gathered in, donkeys were used to thresh the grain, a process that separated the ears of corn from the stalks. "Eeyore" did this simply by crushing the grain under its hooves. Cattle, sheep, and goats were used, too. It was no wonder that the Egyptians were so enthusiastic about their hard-working helpers. *"When there is work to do, get a donkey,"* said an Egyptian proverb.

There was one other important helper that Egyptian farmers could call on to save their aching muscles. This was not an animal, but a clever invention called a "shaduf" that was vital when it came to watering the fields. It looked just like a seesaw: an upright post on which a beam balanced.

The beam had a bucket on one end and a weight on the other. The shaduf was used to lift water out of the river or canal into a ditch to water the fields. Working the shaduf was tiring. The *"arms and neck ache,"* as one writer remarked sadly. But using the shaduf was still much easier than having to raise water entirely by hand.

Crops as abundant as sand

Egyptian farming was very productive, thanks to the great Nile River. Each year the fields yielded not one crop, but two. The grain crop was the first, producing wheat and barley. When this was harvested, there was time to plant and gather in another crop, such as beans, peas, or lentils. Other foods were grown, too – onions, lettuce, cucumber, garlic, and all sorts of fruit. As one contemporary put it, the crops were *"as abundant as the sand."* In a desert country like Egypt, that was really saying something.

Animal magic

Herdsmen were always on the move, leading their masters' animals. Often they went short of food. Look at this thin man with his kilt tucked up. A herdsman frequently carried a stick and a roll of matting to protect himself from the wind and sun.

In addition to growing crops, the Egyptians kept livestock: cattle, sheep, goats, pigs, and poultry. Rich individuals, and wealthy institutions such as the temples, kept very large herds. One nobleman named Renni, for example, left an account of how he had been out in his fields to look at the animals: 1500 pigs, 1200 goats, 100 sheep, and 122 head of cattle. Cattle were especially valuable. They were given names, like the cow called "Good Flood" after the life-giving Nile. Special workers were needed to look after the livestock as they wandered in the fields. Their expertise with the animals was backed up by special magical skills. Charms and magic gestures that were meant to protect the cattle were as much a part of life in the fields as watering the crops.

THE DESERT

There was one place the Egyptians feared more than any other: the desert. There were many reasons for their fears. Here, a royal official spoke of the fear of intruders heading across the desert into Egypt:

The patrol on the edge of the desert has returned and reported: "We have found the tracks of 32 men and three donkeys."

The Red Land

Desert hemmed the Egyptians in, as farming land along the Nile valley soon faded into inhospitable sand. Thinking of the color of its rocks and sand, the Egyptians named it "Deshret" – the "Red Land." Our word "desert" comes from this Egyptian name. Whereas the Black Land stood for everything the Egyptians thought was good, the Red Land was exactly the opposite. It was where the dead were buried. It was a place where nothing grew. *"The desert is dying of famine,"* as one official of Pharaoh Ammenemes III (1844–1797 B.C.) put it. It was a place where wild beasts such as lions were at home. It was also where evil spirits were thought to live, as well as gods intent on upsetting human beings, like the great god Seth. And as we saw at the beginning of this chapter, it was where enemy intruders might enter the kingdom. For most people, the desert was definitely a place to avoid.

Burials took place in the desert because good farming land was too valuable to use for this purpose. Here, you can see the pyramids built for three pharaohs in the desert at Giza: Khufu (2551–2528 B.C.), Khephren (2520–2494 B.C.) and Menkaure (2490–2472 B.C.).

A natural frontier

As much as the Egyptians hated and feared the Red Land, being surrounded by desert did have its advantages. It served as a natural frontier, giving protection from neighboring lands. To the north and east lay sea: the Mediterranean in the north and the Red Sea in the east. Like the desert, the sea helped cut Egypt off from foreign countries. These barriers posed problems for all but the most determined invaders.

The desert was a good place for hunting, as this picture of the young Pharaoh Tutankhamen (1333–1323 B.C.) shows.

Soldiers cross the desert

Because of these natural barriers, it was very unusual for Egypt to be conquered and ruled by foreigners. The years 1640–1532 B.C. were one period of foreign influence, when Egyptian kings lost their grip on the land and were replaced by rulers called the "Hyksos" (which means "rulers of foreign lands.") But by 1532 B.C. the Egyptians were again in control, and determined never to lose power again. The pharaohs who followed were great warriors, kings such as Tuthmosis III (1479–1425 B.C.) and Ramses II (1290–1224 B.C.). They set up a large, specially trained army and used it to win power over foreign peoples in Syria, Palestine, and Asia Minor. This time it was Egyptian soldiers who crossed the desert and created an empire.

Riches from the Red Land

Winning an empire brought great riches to pharaoh. When Tuthmosis III defeated the kingdom of Mitanni in Syria at the Battle of Megiddo in 1456 B.C., he carried away 724 chariots, 2,041 horses, 200 suits of armor, more than 20,000 sheep, and other valuable booty.

But crossing the desert to win battles was not the only way to win riches. Trade was another. Pharaoh regularly sent out trading expeditions. The land of Nubia to the south was especially important for trade. Many exotic and valuable goods were brought into Egypt this way. One scribe listed these items: *"gold, leopard and animal skins, giraffe tails and skins."*

The desert itself produced riches. All sorts of natural resources there were exploited. Rocks were quarried for building, and valuable metal deposits such as gold, copper, and lead were mined. Here, too, pharaoh directed operations. Gold mining made pharaoh Seti I (1306–1290 B.C.) particularly enthusiastic. He ordered tracks to be set up to help bring gold across the desert, and made arrangements for miners and other workers to obtain water and supplies. *"Now that the paths are open and the road is good, gold can be brought back as our lord and master commanded,"* recorded one ancient Egyptian inscription.

This mortuary temple was built for Queen Hatshepsut (1473–1458 B.C.) so that religious rituals for her spirit could be carried out after she died. You can see the desert cliffs very clearly in this picture. They form a natural rock pyramid above her temple, but her actual tomb was hidden, buried in the valley behind.

THE QUARRY

The starting point for the Egyptians' ambitious building projects was the quarry where stone was dug. Herodotus, the ancient Greek, described the bustle and activity when pharaoh Khufu (2551–2528 B.C.) gave orders to build a pyramid at Giza:

Everyone had to work. Some people had to drag stones from the quarries in the Arabian hills to the Nile.

Breaking new ground

By building in stone, the Egyptians were breaking new ground. Ordinary houses were built using mud bricks, which were cheap and easy to make. Using stone meant much more work and a great deal of organization – not to mention a huge workforce to cut stone at the quarries, transport it wherever it was needed, and then do the building. There was only one person who was powerful and wealthy enough to direct operations on this scale – pharaoh.

All the land of Egypt belonged to pharaoh, so his officials were able to go anywhere to pick the best

Moving stone without machinery was work on an epic scale. This picture shows how it was done. An enormous statue has been mounted on a sledge. At the statue's feet, a laborer pours water on to the ground to make the sledge slide more easily. A large gang of men pulls it.

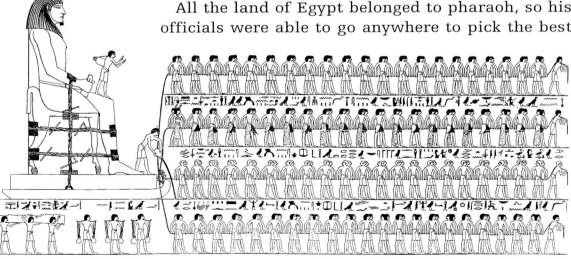

stone for building. In one place there was fine white limestone, just right for the outer surfaces of pyramids. Elsewhere there was sandstone, which could be used for temples, and granite – ideal for making a sarcophagus (ornate coffin). Wherever there was valuable stone, pharaoh could send men out on expeditions to quarry it. When pharaoh Ramses IV (1163–1156 B.C.) wanted building stone, for example, he sent off an expedition of 130 stone masons to cut the stone, along with 800 enslaved prisoners from Asia and 2,000 servants to transport it, and 5,000 soldiers, 50 guards and 170 officials to supervise the expedition. These figures will give you an impression of the colossal amount of work involved in quarrying and building with stone in ancient Egypt.

At the quarry

Quarrying relied on a few simple tools and a good deal of sheer hard work. First, the rock was heated and then cold water was splashed on it. This made the stone more brittle, which helped to break it away from the rock face. Next, the rock was marked into blocks, and cut with a copper chisel and stone hammer. This was skilled work. Other skilled workers were busy with different tasks: chipping the first rough shape of a statue from its stone block, or smoothing stone to prepare it for building. As much work as possible was done at the quarry to make the next back-breaking stage – moving the stone – a little easier.

A *pharaoh's head, carved out of granite. Statues and sculptures such as these were cut out of blocks of stone. They were worked on at the quarry until they were as nearly finished as possible, so that surplus stone did not have to be transported.*

From quarry to Nile

This was where the unskilled workers, like Ramses IV's enslaved prisoners, came into their own. Workers loaded the stone on to wooden sledges and hauled them across the ground to the Nile River. Water was poured on the ground to help

This picture shows the famous Great Sphinx – a beast with a lion's body and a human head. It was carved out of a stone outcrop near the pyramids of Giza.

the sledge slide along. Apart from that, it was all up to the workers. As one block of stone could weigh up to 15 tons, and a statue 60 tons, you can see why quarrying involved such large numbers of laborers.

Once the stone reached the Nile, the quarry-worker's life became a little easier. The sledges with their heavy loads were put on board ship and sailed to their destination. Carved pictures from one pyramid tell the story of one journey like this. *"Delivery of granite columns from the quarries of Elephantine to the pyramid,"* the inscription proudly relates.

All the king's men

Like the quarry-workers, the men who took charge of the stone blocks when they arrived at the building site were pharaoh's workers. They were called up to work on a special project such as building a temple or a pyramid. Skilled men did the fine work; for example, fitting the blocks which made the outer casing of the pyramids. Meanwhile, unskilled workers did more strenuous work, building ramps to lift stone to the higher levels of the pyramid.

THE TOMB

Ancient Egyptians thought a good deal about how they wanted to be buried. They wanted to be surrounded by everything they had needed while they were alive. A tomb such as the one described here was every Egyptian's ideal:

Well set up is the place of eternity, the everlasting tomb. It is filled with offerings and food. It holds every good thing.

Living on

The Egyptians believed in life after death. They thought that various spirits lived in the human body, and that when someone died, these spirits were set free. The most important spirits were the "ka" and the "ba." These spirits were thought to live on forever.

Here, we look into the tomb of Tutankhamen (1333–1323 B.C.). See how the walls are decorated. To make these drawings, the tomb walls were carefully plastered. Then a grid pattern of squares was drawn on the walls, to guide the artists as they painted the outlines. Next, the outlines and background were filled with paint.

Perilous spirit journey

But the ka and the ba did not have an easy journey to the afterlife. First of all, the body they lived in had to be preserved. From about 2,600 B.C. onward, dead bodies were preserved as mummies for just this reason. Then there were tests and dangers that the dead person had to go through on the way to the afterlife. One of these was judgment before the great god of the underworld, Osiris. This trial was called the "weighing of the heart." Into one pan of a pair of scales went the dead person's heart. Into the other went a feather representing the goddess of order and justice, Maat. The gods then reviewed the dead person's life, listening to his or her protests of innocence: *"I have not done evil. I have not done what the gods detest. I have not killed. I have not taken other people's land."* Ammit, the "Eater of the Dead" (a cross between a crocodile, lion, and hippopotamus), was waiting to eat the heart of anyone who failed the test.

People who passed the test could go on to the next stages in the journey to the afterlife. They had to identify the gods and demons and places on the way. According to "The Book of the Dead": *"'I will not open for you," says the bolt of this door, "unless you say my name." [The reply should be] "Toe of his*

The Egyptians thought that death was the start of an important adventure. The spirit of the dead person faced frightening ordeals. We can see one taking place here. The heart of a princess is being weighed to see if it is fit for the afterlife. Hearts that failed the test were eaten by Ammit, a crocodile-headed god.

Mother is your name." Secret magic information like this was the key to success.

The spirits that managed to make their way safely through all these perils would at last be rewarded by life in a land of plenty called the "Fields of Reeds." Here, life would be just like life in Egypt – only better. *"He shall come at last to the Fields of Reeds. Bread, wine, cakes, fields and land shall be given him,"* explained the scribes.

Houses for eternity

To house their bodies for eternity, the Egyptians built many different types of tombs. At first, bodies were simply buried in graves along with tools, pots, and other items that were expected to be useful in the afterlife. Poor people went on being buried like this.

After about 2920 B.C., tombs known as "mastabas" were built for wealthy people. These had underground chambers filled with everything the dead could possibly want, from furniture to cosmetics, and from meals of pigeon stew to jars of wine. The chambers were topped by a mud-brick slab roof above ground. A mastaba also had a chapel above ground, known as a mortuary chapel. Here, food and drink were brought to the spirit of the deceased by his or her family, and by the priests.

Pyramids were grand tombs built for the pharaohs and their families. The first ones developed from the mastabas. The "step pyramid" of Pharaoh Djoser (2630–2611 B.C.), for example, was like six mastabas built on top of each other.

Tombs were also built by cutting deep into desert cliffs. The most famous ones were built in the Valley of the Kings for the royal family and their courtiers after about 1504 B.C. Here, pharaohs such as Tutankhamen (1333–1323 B.C.) and Ramses II (1290–1224 B.C.) were buried in magnificently painted tombs.

This little figure is a model of a servant, placed in the tomb of a wealthy person. Such models were supposed to come to life and help the spirits of the dead by doing all sorts of work for them in the afterlife.

THE PYRAMID

It was believed that pharaoh joined the gods when he died. One contemporary, describing the death of Pharaoh Senwosret I (1971–1926 B.C.), put it like this:

The king of Upper and Lower Egypt flew to heaven and united with the sun disc.

This belief meant it was tremendously important to protect pharaoh's body when he died. Only the biggest, most splendid tomb would do for this: a pyramid.

Changing shapes

Building a tomb was one of the most important projects in any pharaoh's reign. The most spectacular of all royal tombs were the pyramids. These were built at a time in Egyptian history

Carpenters hard at work finishing coffins. The coffins in this picture are "anthropoid" – which means "human-shaped." The lid of a coffin usually carried idealized portraits of the deceased.

that historians call the "Old Kingdom" (2575–2134 B.C.).

The shape of the pyramids developed gradually. At first, they were shaped like flights of steps. The "step pyramid" built for Pharaoh Djoser (2630–2611 B.C.) at Saqqara, designed by the vizier and architect, Imhotep, was the first one of all. After this type came smooth-sided pyramids. The first one of these was built for Pharaoh Sneferu (2575–2551 B.C.).

Mounting to the gods

Religious beliefs influenced the shape of the pyramids. Step pyramids were designed to give the dead pharaoh's spirit a staircase to the gods. *"A staircase to heaven is laid for the king, so he can go up to heaven on it,"* said one contemporary. Smooth-sided pyramids had a special meaning too. Their sides were meant to represent the sun's rays, to remind everyone of the power of the sun and the sun god, Re, the chief of all Egyptian gods. A special prayer for pharaoh tells us about this belief: *"May heaven strengthen the sun's rays for you, so that you may go up to heaven."*

Here we can see inside a pyramid at Saqqara, built between about 2500 and 2350 B.C. Spells have been cut into the stone of the walls. They are among various texts known as "Pyramid Texts." These covered a range of subjects, such as helping to guide the deceased on the journey to the afterlife.

Pyramids and other buildings

A complex of buildings surrounded each pyramid. A special temple called a "mortuary temple" was one of the most important neighboring buildings. Here, daily offerings of food and drink were made to the spirit of the dead king, for the dead were thought to need nourishment, just like the living. A causeway led from the pyramid down to another temple by the Nile. This is where pharaoh's body was received on its way for burial. At Djoser's step pyramid, there was also a great courtyard, built all around the pyramid, for special ceremonial purposes. As for the pyramid itself, a warren of passageways inside led to pharaoh's burial chamber underground. Alongside the chamber were rooms crowded with his belongings.

Counting the cost

Pyramid building was an expensive business. Some facts and figures tell the story. Djoser's pyramid, for example, was 203 feet (62 meters) high, with a base measuring 409 feet (125 meters) by 341 feet (104 meters). The biggest of all pyramids belonged to Pharaoh Khufu (2551–2528 B.C.). About 2.5 million stone blocks were needed to build this 478-feet (146-meter) tall pyramid. It is thought to have taken up to 20 years to build. Only the richest, most powerful pharaoh could afford the labor-power and time for such a monument. If the country went into decline because the Nile floods were poor, pharaoh too became poor. This seemed to happen at the end of the Old Kingdom, in about 2134 B.C., when pyramid building came to an end.

The earliest pyramids had steps, as this one does. The steps were supposed to help the spirit of the dead pharaoh climb to the heavens. Pyramids were surrounded by many other buildings, temples, and walls. This pyramid was surrounded by a wall 32 feet (10 meters) high – with 13 false entrances and only one true one.

Wonders of the world

Egypt's pyramids are regarded as some of the wonders of the world. The more we know about how they were built, the more amazing they seem. Sheer determination and hard work were the main factors, for the builders had no lifting gear such as pulleys and winches to raise stone as the pyramid grew higher. Instead they built great ramps of sand and rubble, then pulled the stone up these and into place. Pyramid builders aimed to build for all eternity, and their work has stood the test of time; the remains of more than 80 pyramids survive today.

THE TEMPLE

One of the best things an Egyptian king could do for his people was to build a temple in honor of the gods. Here, one pharaoh described his temple at Thebes:

It was built to last for all time, made of fine sandstone. The pavements were made of silver and all the doors of gold.

Worth more than a million soldiers

The Egyptians worshiped many different gods and goddesses. A few gods were worshiped throughout the land. The god Amun, "the hidden one," became linked with the sun god Re, and became very popular. Many people called him "king of the gods." They believed that the gods controlled the universe. A craftsman named Neferabu described the sort of disaster that might happen if they were insulted. He announced, *"I am a man who swore falsely by the god Ptah … He struck me blind."* It was thought that people could avoid disasters like this by worshiping the gods in the right way. *"Amun is worth more to me than a million soldiers,"* declared Ramses II (1290–1224 B.C.).

A statue of the goddess Hathor. Huge statues of gods, goddesses, kings – and sometimes queens – decorated the temples. Their great size was meant to tell people how important they were.

Home of the gods

Worship was centered on temples built the length and breadth of the land. But they were more than just places where the gods were worshiped. People believed that the spirits of the gods actually lived inside special statues in the temples. These statues

25

were treated with great respect. In return, the gods were supposed to do what the king asked them. An inscription in one temple summed up the relations between the Egyptians and their gods, as a sort of bargain: *"The king has come to the god with offerings so that you will give him all lands."*

Secrets, signs, and symbols

Four colossal statues of King Ramses II (1290–1224 B.C.), about 68 feet (21 meters) high, were made to tower above visitors at his temple at Abu Simbel in Nubia. Ramses had seven temples built in Nubia. Temple building was one of the duties a king was expected to perform.

Temples were very dark and secret places. Worship there was carried out by the priests and priestesses, not ordinary people as they were not allowed beyond the first courtyard.

To the Egyptians, the temple buildings themselves had mystical meaning. They were built as small-scale models of the universe. Each temple was surrounded by a high mud-brick wall, hiding the inside from inquisitive outsiders. Inside was a towering gateway known as a "pylon." Sometimes there was a series of pylons. At the temple of Amun at Karnak, for example, six massive pylons were built. They were often carved with pictures of pharaoh triumphant over his enemies. Pictures such as these were not just for decoration. It was believed that they had magic power to make the scenes come alive.

Behind the pylon was a court-yard, and behind this was a roofed hall. In the hall were tall columns topped by carvings of lotus flowers and water plants. These were meant to remind worshipers of an ancient Egyptian creation myth, which told how the world first came into being as a mound of dry land rising out of water.

The first temple ever was supposed to have been built on this dry mound.

As worshipers went into the temple, a feeling of mystery was created as the rooms became narrower, the ceilings lower and the floors higher, until at the very heart of the temple they came to the sanctuary and the god's statue.

The massive monumental gateway (pylon) at the temple dedicated to the god Horus at Edfu. Pictures of the king triumphant over his enemies are cut into the stone.

Offerings – and power

Pharaohs liked to be generous to the temples and give rich offerings to the gods. *"I lavish my goods on your store houses,"* said one king. In this way temples became rich, owning land in many places. The temple of Amun at Karnak, with more than 80,000 workers and 400,000 cattle, was the wealthiest of all the temples. Riches led to power. The temple of Amun, for instance, gradually came to play an important part in government, until in about 1070 B.C., when Egypt was divided and in turmoil, the temple was a controlling force in the south of the country.

THE HOUSE OF LIFE

Centers of learning, known as "Houses of Life," were attached to the most important temples. The words of one royal official show us how highly respected they were:

His Majesty told me to restore the Houses of Life which had fallen into disrepair. I filled them with students and put wise men in charge.

Wise men

Meet Thoth. Thoth was the Egyptian god of wisdom and the god of the scribes – those who worked in the Houses of Life. You can see that Thoth is shown with the head of the ibis bird, which had a beak shaped like a pen.

Houses of Life were like universities, libraries, and book production centers all rolled into one. All sorts of subjects were studied: religion, magic, medicine, mathematics, geometry, astronomy, geography. They were not open to everyone. Priests who worked in the temple were allowed to study, and sometimes outsiders too: but only men, not women.

Learning was looked upon as something secret and mystical by the Egyptians: even being able to read and write was thought to give people special power. Pharaoh often picked advisers from the scribes and priests of the Houses of Life, because of their reputation for wisdom. One story tells how a certain scribe was singled out for pharaoh's special attention because he was so wise *"you could ask him anything."* But the fame of the wise men of the Houses of Life traveled much farther than pharaoh's court. Egypt was known for its learning throughout the ancient world.

Books, books, books

Libraries were a special feature of the Houses of Life. A royal visit to one of these libraries was recorded in this ancient inscription: *"His Majesty went to the House of the Book and opened the writings with his courtiers."* The books that the royal visitors looked at were written by hand, like all books at this time. In Egypt, a marsh plant called papyrus was used as material to write on. Many sheets of papyrus were joined together for long pieces of writing. For storage purposes, papyrus books were wound into rolls.

Scribes studying in the Houses of Life did not just read books. They were also responsible for making more, copying out texts already in the library, so that Egyptian wisdom could be passed on.

In the House of Life, priests and scribes studied Egyptian stories of gods and goddesses. In this painting from the tomb of Horemheb (1319–1307 B.C.), you can see the king standing with the goddess Isis and her son, Horus.

Star gazing

Astronomy, the study of the stars, was a subject the scribes and priests of the Houses of Life were especially famous for – and the flat roofs of the pylons in the temple were particularly good places for star gazing. With their fervent interest in the Nile River and its floods, there was one star that particularly interested the Egyptians. This was the "Dog Star," Sirius. Careful watching showed that Sirius could not be seen all year around. More careful watching showed that it became visible at about the time of year that the Nile flood began. This was regarded as the beginning of a new year. The astronomers' observations provided a valuable forecast for the farmers, as it let them know when to begin to get ready for the flood. In such ways, studying the stars had practical uses for the ancient Egyptians.

THE HOUSE OF LIFE

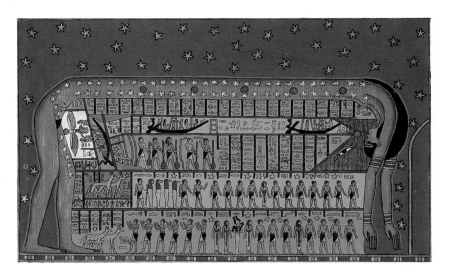

Learning about the stars, Egyptian style. This copy of an Egyptian tomb painting shows the Egyptian view of the sky. In the House of Life, priests and scribes learned how gods and goddesses were thought to be linked with the stars. In this picture, the goddess Nut represents the night sky.

Counting the days

Studying the stars led to one especially important development: working out a calendar. A calendar that tells us how to divide time up into days, months, and years is something we take for granted today. But the Egyptians had to be pioneers and make their own calculations.

Most calendars are based either on the phases of the moon or on the movement of the earth around the sun. Thanks to the priests and scribes in the Houses of Life, the Egyptians were the very first people to work out a calendar based on the sun. This gave them a year of 365.25 days. The year was then divided up into 12 months, and each month was arranged as three ten-day periods. There were five extra days that did not fit the pattern at the end of the year. They were thought to be the birthdays of the gods Osiris, Seth, Horus, Isis, and Nepthys and were holidays. Much later, toward the end of the great period of ancient Egypt, they became known as the "days of the demons" and were days on which everyone expected bad luck. Even the wise men of the Houses of Life took superstitions and myths of this kind very seriously indeed.

THE PALACE

I n about 1350 B.C., Egyptian craftsmen were building a tomb for a high-ranking courtier. They wanted to decorate it with pictures of the most important events of the courtier's life. Naturally, his days at pharaoh's palace had to be included, so on some of the pictures:

The king appeared at the great double doors in his palace. The officials, the king's friends and royal servants were brought in.

The great house

Pharaoh and his family lived in great splendor. In fact, the Egyptian word "per-ao" (pharaoh) means "great house." This tells us that when the Egyptians thought of their king, the magnificence of his surroundings instantly came into their minds.

Many kings had more than one palace. Most were set in important places such as Thebes or Memphis. Others were deliberately built in remote areas so the king could be away from the hustle and bustle. Some palaces were built especially for a particular royal festival. When Pharaoh Amenophis III (1391–1353 B.C.) had ruled Egypt for 30 years, he ordered a new palace near Thebes to celebrate the fact. Inside this palace, the walls were plastered and then painted in bright colors with pictures of various animals, birds, and plants.

To have your own pool was a real luxury. You could stock it with scented lotus flowers, fish and birds, and plant figs, dates, and acacia trees around it.

31

The king's palace was a sign of his power. Important palaces were often linked to a temple, to emphasize this. At Madinet Habu, for example, Ramses III (1194–1163 B.C.) built a temple in the middle of many other royal buildings, to remind everyone that pharaoh was a god.

In very early times, palace walls were built of mud brick and decorated with paneling. This was such a special feature that no one else was allowed to use this building design. If a scribe drew a stretch of wall decorated with paneling, everyone would know that he was writing about the king. This shows how important the palace was. No one could think about the king without thinking about his palace.

From throne room to bathroom

The palace was both a center of government and pharaoh's home. The most important room was the throne room. This is where pharaoh sat to receive official visitors, with his throne raised on a step called a "dais." Officials and important foreign visitors made their way here, bowing low to kiss the ground beneath pharaoh's feet.

On special occasions, the king allowed his people to see him in the "window of appearance" which led from the throne room to a great courtyard. It was the custom for pharaoh to present gifts to his courtiers and officials from this window. Pieces of gold and jewelry were special marks of favor. *"Rewards were given out – ducks and fish made of gold. The people were given ribbons of green linen,"* wrote a contemporary, describing one of these ceremonies.

The largest palaces were surrounded by little buildings where pharaoh's scribes worked, busy keeping records and accounts, writing letters to foreign kings on pharaoh's behalf, and issuing orders to officials all over the kingdom.

A *chair fit for a king. This wooden chair from the tomb of Tutankhamen (1333– 1323 B.C.) is covered in gold and decorated with silver, jewels, colored glass and glazed pottery. It shows Tutankhamen and his wife at home. Imagine how a palace would have looked filled with furniture like this.*

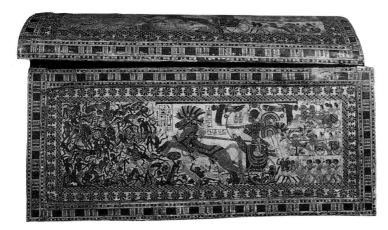

The inscription on this box reads "Sandals for His Majesty. Life, health, strength!" When it was found, after more than 3,500 years in the tomb, it did contain several pairs of Tutankhamen's sandals. Imagine using this as a shoe box!

The palace also contained suites of rooms for pharaoh and his family: finely decorated and richly furnished bedrooms, the harem (women's quarters) and even bathrooms. The royal bathrooms were real marvels in Egyptian eyes. Dirty water drained away through a channel in the floor, but clean water had to be brought in by servants. Not even the palace had running water or sewers.

Parties and pleasure

Pharaoh, his family and courtiers had a much more leisurely life than ordinary people did. The palace thronged with servants, from the "overseer of the royal bathrooms," to the king's sandal-bearer. Entertainers were brought in to *please His Majesty every day in the Great Palace.* There were many banquets, with singers, musicians and dancing girls to greet guests with garlands of flowers. Some palace grounds boasted collections of wild animals, and many had lakes and pleasure grounds. But pharaoh had to be cautious, even in the middle of his pleasure grounds and courtiers, in case anyone was plotting against him. This happened to the powerful Ramses III when some of the women in his harem conspired against him, although the plot was discovered and the conspirators were then put on trial.

THE FACTORY

In about 2040 B.C., a scribe sat down to describe what it was like to do other people's jobs, and why it was really best to be a scribe. This is what he said about one of the many big workshops in the country, a metal workshop:

I have seen the blacksmith at his task, at the mouth of his furnace. His fingers were like the skin of crocodiles, and he stank ... worse than fish eggs.

No time to be lazy

There were many different craftsmen in Egypt – including potters, jewelers, metalworkers, carpenters, glassmakers, leatherworkers, clothmakers, and artists. They were all kept busy: from the gold-plated throne in pharaoh's palace and the elegant ebony chairs in a noble family's house, to the wooden hair comb in the humblest worker's home, everything that the Egyptians needed had to be made by hand. There was no shortage of work for Egypt's craftsmen. On one thing they all agreed: it was hard work. *"The jeweller has to drill hard stones till he is tired and weak,"* the scribe wrote with pity.

Egyptian craftsmen created this little blue hippopotamus. It is made of faience. Glass was used for beads as well as for little figures like this.

Working together

Egyptian craftsmen did not set up in business and work for themselves, selling their work to the public. Instead, their work was organized in large workshops, like little factories. Work involved a good deal of cooperation. Metal workshops, for

34

example, show us how making just one item involved contributions from several different workers. Many metal objects were made by "casting" – pouring hot liquid metal into molds. To do this, unskilled workers were needed to keep the fires going and to pour the liquid metal into the molds. Skilled workers created the molds and added ornamental finishing touches, such as engraving patterns on vases.

No one without a boss

Workshops were owned not by business people but by some of the most important people – and places – in the land. Pharaoh had many workshops attached to his palaces: some for gold making, others for jewelry, wood carving, weaving, wig making and so on. He also controlled other crafts, such as glass-making and papyrus making. High-ranking officials and members of pharaoh's family also owned workshops. So, too, did the temples. The temple of Re at Heliopolis owned five workshops, while the wealthy temple of Amun at Karnak topped this figure with forty-six.

Boatbuilding was a job that required many workers. Here, you can see carpenters setting to work with tools called adzes. They are smoothing down the hull of a boat.

Workshops like these produced goods for their owners to use. Temples wanted painters and other artists to work on pictures and statues of the gods, and weavers to make linen to clothe the statues.

"There's no one without a boss," said the scribe. That was certainly true in the workshops, where the owner had great power. The owners provided the tools and raw materials that their craftsmen needed. In return, they kept the finished products and paid the workers. Sometimes the owner even sent craftsmen to work for someone else for a while. The best ones generally ended up in pharaoh's workshops, but the king sometimes loaned out his top craftsmen as a special favor.

A living wage

Coins were not used in Egypt, so wages were paid in "kind," usually in foodstuffs. Bread and beer were the basics of people's diets, and the main part of the craftsmen's wage. Pharaoh's tomb-builders provided a good example of this. They were given rations of wheat and barley to make bread and beer. From time to time they received a "bonus" – such as meat, blocks of salt, or sesame oil.

Learning the job

With very few exceptions, the workshops were a man's world. Boys usually followed in their father's footsteps. They were taken on as teenagers to work as apprentices (trainees), learning on the job. An apprenticeship lasted for about three years, and ended with the trainee producing a skilled piece of work to prove the ability to work without supervision. Then the apprentice was qualified for a lifetime's work.

A model of pharaoh's workers in the royal brewery. Royal palaces needed workshops such as this to provide them with food and drink.

THE WEAVING SHOP

Everyone in Egypt needed the weavers. It was their job to turn thread into cloth. But if this ancient writer is to be believed, the conditions that weavers endured as they worked at the loom were so uncomfortable that few liked their work:

The weaver in the workshop has a bad time. His knees are pushed up against his chest so he cannot breathe. If he misses a day's work he gets beaten.

Women's work

By and large, weaving was women's work. And to prove it, the hieroglyphic that scribes used to write the word "weaver" was a picture of a woman sitting down, holding a shuttle, one of the tools of the trade. In poor homes it was the women who wove cloth to turn into clothes for the family. Wealthy people employed female servants for this work. Really large-scale establishments such as palaces

Two women spinning thread. Really skillful workers could use two spindles at once, as the woman on the left here is doing.

Guests at a banquet dressed in the height of fashion. White was always the most fashionable color, a sign of wealth and rank.

and temples had special weaving workshops to produce everything they wanted. Sometimes, however, men did work as weavers. More and more men began to fill these jobs after about 1550 B.C.

Work at the weaving shop

The weaving shop was a hive of activity, busy with workers of a wide range of ages, from 12-year-old apprentices upwards. As the quotation at the start of this chapter tells us, work was strictly disciplined, usually carried out under the eagle eye of a supervisor. Taking a few minutes off work was not easy. One source tells us that weavers had to bribe an official with tidbits of food to let them out *"to see the light of day."*

Flax into cloth

The women and men in these workshops helped with almost every step involved in turning flax (a plant) into linen cloth. After some work preparing the flax, drying, soaking, beating, and combing it, the first important task was spinning. This produced good, long threads for the weavers to work with. Spinning was done by hand, using a stick called a spindle, with a weight known as a whorl attached. The flax fibers were joined to the spindle, which was set spinning around and allowed to drop slowly to the floor. As it fell, it twisted the fiber into a long thread. The thread was then picked up and rolled into a ball, and then it was time for the spinner to begin all over again. Really skillful spinners could work two spindles at once.

Weaving was done sitting at a loom. This put together two sets of threads, one running lengthwise and the other crosswise, passing each set over and under the other in turn. Weaving produced cloth. The finished product could be used for almost anything, from the finest, most fashionable clothes to the linen bandages used for wrapping mummies. When you know that it could take more than 4,035 square feet (375 square meters) of cloth to wrap just one mummy, you will realize that cloth was always in demand.

Put on fine linen

For peasants and poor people, clothes were simple and workaday. A man wore a linen cloth around the waist, folded as a sort of kilt, and a woman wore a dress. Wealthier people, however, could afford to be fashion-conscious. When one poet wanted to advise readers on how to enjoy themselves, wearing elegant clothes was high on the list. *"Put on fine linen,"* he urged. Linen so fine it was almost transparent, folded in pleats and bleached whiter than white, was the very height of fashion. Color was provided by beads and jewelry, worn by men as well as women. Wigs were also fashionable. These were usually made from human hair. They were always worn at parties and banquets, but they had another purpose, too – to protect people's heads from the sun.

This wooden spoon, carved to look like a servant woman, was made for pouring out perfume. The Egyptians were very fond of perfume. For special banquets, courtiers wore wigs topped with cones of perfumed animal fat. The fat gradually melted in the heat, releasing its fragrance as it trickled down the wig.

THE MARKET

Going shopping in Egypt was a noisy, hectic, time-consuming business – and pictures on the walls of one official's tomb in Saqqara tell us all about it. They show a market in progress, with traders and their wares thronging the street. Inscriptions give a flavor of the conversation going on all around. One trader says:

Give me some of your beer, and I'll give you sweet vegetables.

No money

In ancient times the Egyptians managed to do without money. There were no coins. Going shopping, paying taxes to pharaoh, paying wages to servants and craftsmen: every activity you can think of took place without money changing hands. This didn't put a stop to business – not a bit of it. If you look again at the tomb inscription at the

Geese like these were brought to market for sale. They were eaten at banquets, and were usually on the shopping lists of only wealthy Egyptians.

beginning of this chapter, you will see how the economy worked without coins. An Egyptian lady who explained how she was able to afford to hire servants gives us another clue. *"I bought them in exchange for garden produce,"* she declared. This evidence tells us that the Egyptians operated a system of swaps instead of using money. Historians call this exchange system "barter."

Going shopping

Shopping was very different from today. For one thing, there was much less to buy – no consumer goods such as videos, for example. Most food was made at home, and instead of having shops stocked with racks of clothes and goods for people to browse through, the Egyptians either made their own, or placed an order with

The market was a place where buyers and sellers drove bargains with each other. Here you can see two people who might make a deal.

local craftsmen. For the Egyptians, shopping meant making a swap with someone you knew, or going to a town or large village with an outdoor market.

Everyone turned up at market – local people such as farmers, craftsmen, fishermen, even housewives who had baked some extra bread to swap. There were traders and craftsmen from other places too, who traveled about with wares to sell, such as beads, cloth, mirrors, razors, eye paint, and jars for cosmetics. For hungry shoppers, stalls were set up to sell beer and snacks.

Fixing a price

Going shopping used up a good deal of energy, because prices were always negotiable; the seller would try to drive a hard bargain, while the buyer tried to push the price down. But although there were no fixed prices, people had a special way of working out what things were worth. This made bartering fairly straightforward.

Metal, such as copper, silver, and gold, was especially valuable. It was valued by weight: the heavier the bit of metal, the more valuable it was. So the Egyptians decided to set other prices in terms of fixed metal weights. The "deben," a copper weight of about .5 ounce (14 grams), was the key to most prices. A pair of shoes or a razor cost one or two deben; a pig five deben; and a coffin more than 20 deben. People wanting to buy a coffin would either have to come up with 20 deben of copper for the carpenter, or goods worth 20 deben – four pigs, for example.

Exchanges with other lands

Egypt was so renowned for its wealth that pharaoh sometimes received requests for presents of gold from kings in foreign lands. They were confident that he had so much that he could easily spare a little for them.

Egyptian rulers were interested in the riches to be had from other countries, too. Trading expeditions with royal escorts were sent out on many occasions. One of the most famous was despatched by Queen Hatshepsut (1473–1458 B.C.) to bring back exotic and valuable spices such as myrrh and frankincense from a destination known as the "land of Punt." Scenes of the expedition were carved at the temple built for her tomb at Deir el-Bahri near Thebes. Trade with Africa was also important. This was channeled through the land of Nubia, Egypt's neighbor to the south. Baboons, ostrich feathers, and pygmies were on pharaoh's shopping list here.

Today we expect countries to trade with each other and have a money-based relationship. In ancient times, things were different. This scene of Nubians bringing wild animals as tribute to pharaoh's court tells us something about this. Paying tribute was a way of recognizing another country's importance – and a way that goods were passed from one land to another.

THE HOUSE

When Egyptians had to describe their ideal home, the gardens outside were almost as important to them as the inside, as these words tell us:

The house is pleasant to live in. There are fishes and waterbirds in its pools.

Making a pleasant home

Great or small, Egyptian houses were built of mud bricks. The walls were plastered, inside and out, and then whitewashed. Windows were small, set high up in the walls, making the inside of the house cool and rather dark. The roof was flat, surrounded by a parapet, with a flight of stairs providing access to it. These roofs provided storage space, and somewhere cooler to get away to at night.

The Egyptians were sociable people who liked to give parties and banquets in their homes. Musicians such as these women could be hired to provide entertainment on these occasions.

This pottery model of an Egyptian house was made for the spirit of a dead person to live in during the afterlife. For this reason, it is called a "soul house." The model tells us about the sort of house poorer people lived in. On the left, an archway leads to stairs up to the roof. The flat roof added useful extra living space.

Archaeologists investigating a village called Deir el-Medina near Thebes, built especially for pharaoh's tomb-builders in about 1500 B.C., have been able to find out a good deal about ordinary people's houses. In this village, all the houses were built to one basic design. Opening straight on to the street, each house was long and narrow, with four main rooms. First came a hall, then the main living room, next a bedroom or storeroom, and then a kitchen at the back of the house. There were cellars underground for storage.

Wealthy people had larger houses than the tomb-builders did, but the basic elements were the same. Special luxuries included a spacious courtyard surrounded by high, colorfully painted walls. In the center lay a pool, where fish swam and lotus flowers grew. Shade was provided next to the house by a covered arcade, supported by painted wooden pillars carved in the form of papyrus stalks and lotus buds.

Looking inside

The houses of working people had little furniture. The floor was for sitting on, and mats for sleeping on. Wealthy people could afford elegant furniture made by craftsmen. But even in their homes there were fewer pieces of furniture and decorations than we would expect today. Chairs were rarities, signs that the owner was someone important. Meals were often served on mats on the floor rather than on tables. The bedroom was furnished with a wooden bed, a headrest made of wood or stone instead of a pillow, perhaps a stool, and chests and baskets for clothes and personal possessions. No one in Egypt, not even pharaoh, had a house with running water or any kind of waste system. There were toilets of a kind – wooden stools with a hole in the middle and a pot underneath. These pots needed to be regularly emptied outside.

Family life

Houses were meant for family life: there were no houses where just one person lived. Today in the West, many houses have just four inhabitants: two parents and two children. In Egypt, many houses had at least six inhabitants, and often more. Parents, children, a widowed grandmother, unmarried aunts, and other relatives would live together, packed under one roof.

Children were brought up to respect older people, especially their parents. Girls rarely received an academic education unless they were princesses, but some boys were taught to read and write. Childhood ended at about the age of ten, when boys and girls were expected to make themselves useful. Boys helped their fathers; with farmers' sons helping in the fields and herdsmen's sons helping with the cattle, for example. Girls helped their mothers around the house.

An Egyptian sits down to while away some time playing a popular board game called "senet."

Before this age, children had time to play. Archaeologists have discovered many Egyptian toys – for instance, little animals made out of baked mud, such as hippos and crocodiles, wooden dolls, boardgames, balls, whips, and tops. These were all treasured possessions, and signs that life in ancient Egyptian places had many moments of fun.

GLOSSARY

Amun The chief state-god of Egypt. Usually associated with Re, the sun god, and also called Amun-Re.

Architect An important royal official in charge of a building project.

Ba One of the spirit parts of a person, like the soul, thought to live on after death.

Black Land Area that the Nile River flooded and covered with black mud each year, making good farming land.

Deben A copper weight used to fix prices.

Fields of Reeds Place of happiness where the dead went to live forever.

Hieroglyphics Egyptian system of writing using picture signs. It was very elaborate and required much careful practice.

Horus A god with a human body and the head of a hawk. He was the son of Osiris and identified with the living pharaoh.

House of Life Place of learning attached to an important temple.

Inscription Words cut in stone, often recording important events.

Irrigation A system to drain and control river and floodwater.

Isis A goddess, the wife and sister of the god Osiris.

Ka One of the spirit parts of a person, like a "double," thought to live on after death.

Lower Egypt The north of Egypt, joined to the south in about 3000 B.C.

Mastaba A type of tomb, with a flat roof and mud-brick walls.

Mortuary chapel A chapel built at a tomb. Offerings of food and drink were made here to the spirit of the dead person.

Mortuary temple A temple associated with a tomb (usually royal).

Mummy A dead body that had been dried out, treated with preservatives, and wrapped in linen bandages.

Osiris An important Egyptian god, thought to rule the land of the dead.

Papyrus (plural **papyri**) A reed, or a sheet of writing material made from the reed.

Pharaoh King of the Egyptians.

Pylon A monumental gateway in a temple.

Pyramid A style of tomb built for a member of the royal family.

Re One of the names of the sun god.

Red Land The desert.

Sarcophagus (plural **sarcophagi**) An elaborate coffin.

Scribe A man who could write; he worked keeping records and accounts.

Shaduf A device to lift water from a river or canal to water fields.

Step pyramid A pyramid shaped like a flight of steps.

Upper Egypt The south of Egypt, joined to the north in about 3000 B.C.

Vizier Pharaoh's chief official.

FURTHER READING

Corbishley, Mike, *Pathways: Timelines of the Ancient World*, Macdonald Young Books, 1995.

Defrates, Joanna, *What Do We Know About Egyptians?*, Macdonald Young Books, 1994.

Hart, George, *Eyewitness Ancient Egypt*, Dorling Kindersley, 1990.

Howarth, Sarah, *The Unfolding World – The Pyramid Builders*, Quarto/Running Press 1993.

The Visual Dictionary of Ancient Civilizations, Dorling Kindersley, 1994.

INDEX